THE LITTLE BOOK OF BAD BUSINESS ADVICE

by Steve Altes

St. Martin's Paperbacks

THE LITTLE BOOK OF BAD BUSINESS ADVICE

Copyright © 1997 by Steve Altes.

ISBN: 0-312-96223-1

Printed in the United States of America

St. Martin's Paperbacks edition/June 1997

10 9 8 7 6 5 4 3 2 1

DEDICATION

Dedicated to anyone who has ever picked up a
book of business advice and said, "Duh!"

ACKNOWLEDGMENTS

Thanks to Baroness Sheri de Borchgrave, Jennifer Enderlin, Amy Kolenik, Shannon McKenna, Edmund Pendleton, Matt Terrigno, and Kirsten Hebbe for their contributions. Special thanks to my parents, Stephen and Doris Altes who—this book notwithstanding—always give me the best advice.

iNTRODUCTiON

Save us from the hordes of management consultants and self-styled experts who purport to have great insight into the business world. Every day somebody publishes a new book with a title like "You Win, I Win, We All Win," "How to Manage A Butthead," and "Goal-Setting: Your Key to Everlasting Career Success."

Football coaches, real estate moguls, even Attila the Hun and Winnie-the-Pooh are peddling business advice books.

Pick up these books and you'll be astonished to learn that people don't like a limp handshake, that communication skills are important, and that you have to take risks to get ahead. Contemplate the meaning of sage advice like "If you're going to sell

ice to Eskimos, make sure it's really good ice."
Good luck!

Look, business isn't so difficult. Phoenician traders had it all figured out thousands of years ago and the basic principles haven't changed. It's all just common sense. So put down your Day-Timer, America. Stop updating your "Five-Year Career/Life Plan" long enough to read this book. It's the last business book you'll ever need.

1. Never answer phones promptly. You don't want to appear too desperate for business.

2. Flirt with people at work. You might get a raise, you might get sex—either way, you can't lose.

3. When entering other employees' offices, greet them with a loud, "What the hell are you doing!?"

4. **Breeze past top executives' secretaries by always insisting your calls are "personal, confidential, and extremely urgent."**

☎

5. **When leaving voice-mail messages, talk v...e...r...y...s...l...o...w... l...y and repeat yourself a lot. Until you leave your phone number. Thentalkveryfast.**

6. **Park in the visitors' lot.**

7. **Customers, though fond of waiting, are rarely right.**

8. **Use expense reports to give yourself a nice little bonus. You know the top dogs do.**

9. **If they didn't want you making a bunch of personal phone calls, they shouldn't have put a phone on your desk.**

10. **Follow your brother-in-law's hot stock tip.**

11. Watch SpectraVision soft-core porn movies in your hotel room and charge 'em to the company.

12. Institute a new form, policy, or procedure every week.

13. Advertise your ambition. Keep a folder in plain sight on your desk labeled "Stuff I'll Change as Soon as They Put Me in Charge of This Dump."

14. Do what you love. Poverty will follow.

☎

15. Earn extra income by running a side business from your office like knitting Norwegian sweaters, dog-sitting, or operating a phone sex line.

16. Avoid excessive eye contact with people. It gives them the creeps.

17. **If you must work late, rummage through the refrigerator. There *is* such a thing as a free lunch.**

18. **Never mind the corporate travel policy. Fly whatever airline gives you the best frequent-flyer miles.**

19. **Read other people's faxes while waiting for your fax to go through. It's a good way to stay abreast of their activities without having to listen to them drone on in staff meetings.**

20. Shoot the messenger.

21. Earn a fearsome reputation among colleagues by periodically calling the weather recording and launching into a blistering diatribe about some imaginary topic.

22. Read viewgraph charts verbatim.

23. People only read the beginning and the end of memos, so in the middle of a really long memo, put in a sentence like, "Thus, as the preceding analysis indicates, letting the chimpanzee drive the sports car over the mountain pass was probably not wise of Jim even under the best of road conditions," to see if anyone is paying attention.

24. Set aside a few minutes every day to yell at your boss.

25. **When you hire someone, explain that you see it as less of an employment contract and more as a "buying of their soul."**

26. **Cheat on your taxes. Everyone else does.**

27. **Do a parody of your boss at the company talent show. Screw him if he can't take a joke.**

28. **In today's litigious society, protect yourself by having a team of lawyers review every outgoing business letter.**

29. **Think of work as a free office supply store that serves coffee.**

30. **Minesweeper and Solitaire—two great ways to improve your hand-mouse dexterity.**

31. **Leave memos on people's chairs, never in their in-box.**

32. No one notices your scuffed shoes or ratty old briefcase.

33. Make yourself seem more educated by speaking in Shakespearean lingo: "But soft, good lady, methinks 'tis folly the marketing plan thou doth advocate," or "Rebuked is thy budget. 'Tis the work of a knave and a rascal!"

34. Never let your career interfere with your hobbies.

35. When you win a difficult negotiation, savor the experience by gloating over your adversary.

36. Pontificate, criticize, and argue.

37. Practice the expression, "Oh, is it Secretary's Day? I completely forgot."

38. **Adopt endearing eccentricities to stand out from the crowd. For example, after receiving someone's business card, rip it in half and say, "That's all right. I'll just call you Joe Blow. It's easier for me to remember."**

39. **In job interviews, speak ill of your former bosses.**

40. **Becoming department head before you reach forty is the only true guarantee of happiness in this world.**

41. **Reinvent the wheel.**

42. **In lieu of Christmas gifts, send clients a card saying that a donation has been made in their name to "The Society to Maim Helpless Animals."**

43. **When coworkers bore you with stories about how adorable their children are, break in with, "Yeah, yeah, that's nothing. I had a gerbil once and no snot-nosed ankle-biter can compare to him."**

44. Have a good cry at the office at least once a week.

45. Your job is to identify problems. Let the rest of them worry about solving them.

46. Take candy from other people's desks, but never bring your own.

47. Over thirty-five? Hope you're happy because you're too old to start over or try anything new.

48. While away the hours by flipping through office supply catalogs and ordering various walnut-laminated plastic gizmos.

49. Adopt a memorable company motto like: "You could do business with our competitors . . . but you'd be a real nimrod if you did!" or "We may not be the best in town, but there's no one costlier!" or "Buy our product! It's more fun than driving red-hot pokers into your eyeballs!"

50. Win the affection of the corporate finance people by calling them "those darn bean counters."

51. Look the other way when passing people in the hall to avoid having to say "Hi" to them constantly.

52. Always explain your job in terms that your mother would not understand.

53. Show you are worldly by using foreign words in business meetings. *E.g., entre nous*, I don't know whether Debbie's *magnum opus* is a *pièce de résistance* or simply *pro forma*. Let's have a *tête-à-tête mañana*.

54. Interrupt people if they talk too slowly in meetings.

55. The company Christmas party—spirits are high, you're feeling uninhibited—no better time to ask the boss for a raise.

56. Endear yourself to colleagues by calling them cute nicknames like "Little Miss Swivel Hips," "Cro-Magnon Man," or "Poo Breath."

☎

57. Tell coworkers, "That's not how we did it at my old company!" at least once a day.

58. Ask the CEO if she will commit to mentoring you for a few hours every day.

59. Put a fanciful title on your business card like "Marketing Czar," "Grand Poobah," or "Engineering Wizard."

60. Think of your résumé as a creative writing exercise. Like they're really going to call Harvard and check up on you.

61. It's not *who* you know, silly! It's *what* you know!

62. **Don't kid yourself. Rejection of your work is a rejection of you. Take it personally.**

63. **Never mind what the market will bear, base your price to sell something on how much it costs you to make.**

64. **Booze it up during business lunches.**

65. **End every business meeting with the admonition, "Remember, we never had this discussion."**

66. **Employees only care about themselves. Treat them with suspicion.**

☎

67. **Ask your staff if they are familiar with the term "spanking a memo." Make up a description to go with this term. Ask that it be done to all memos before they are sent to you.**

68. **On "Family Day" encourage your kids to play with other employees' computers.**

69. **Befriend the mailroom guys. If they like you, they'll let you push a lot of personal mail and FedExes through the system.**

70. **Never have an agenda for a meeting. Let it free-flow.**

71. **Keep pesky refrigerator prowlers at bay by writing on your lunch bag, "Tissue Sample—Biohazard."**

72. **Use jargon and technobabble.**

73. **Dress in whatever makes you feel the most productive, be it jeans, sweats, or a long, flowing cape.**

74. **Allow your staff one expense report per year. Tell them they must float their expenses for twelve months.**

75. **Be known as "the office gossip."**

76. When a project gets in trouble, call an all-hands meeting and announce that you will now begin "The Search for The Guilty."

77. Take continuing education courses in "Micromanagement."

78. Leave fake phone messages to yourself for others to accidentally see and be impressed, like "CEO wants you to call him at home tonight regarding corporate strategy."

79. Don't contribute to 401(k) plans. They're a rip-off.

80. Refuse your company's Employee Handbook and proclaim: "This is fine for lemmings like you who can't use the john without instructions. I play by my own rule book. Get used to it."

81. Make cellular phone calls in the middle of business lunches.

82. **Dance all around your company's product name. Avoid saying it at all costs. If someone says it, say "Please don't mention that filthy word."**

83. **Only wussies back-up their data. Take a walk on the wild side.**

84. **Giving employees performance evaluations is a fruitless waste of time. They know how they're doing.**

85. When giving presentations, slouch, mumble, and say "um" a lot.

86. When colleagues are working late at the office, ask them if there is anything you can do to help, like going to their homes and sleeping with their spouses, that sort of thing.

87. Answer your phone with the greeting, "Speak, supplicant."

88. **In business writing, use phrases like "obviously" and "as you can clearly see" a lot.**

89. **Avoid risk and change. It causes trouble.**

90. **Cheat at the company softball game. It shows management you have what it takes to get ahead in this dog-eat-dog world.**

91. **Sign contracts without reading them.**

92. On the anniversary of your hiring date, wear all black and tell people it's to commemorate "the death of your spirit."

93. Wear bow ties to look smarter.

94. Send your boss a weekly evaluation of how well she is managing you.

95. **Every time you open your paycheck envelope, do a double-take, and shout, "Jimminy Christmas, this is a lot of money. I can't believe they've given me another raise!"**

96. Save paper by printing memos in font size 8.

97. **When customers call with questions about your product, a firm "Have you ever thought about reading the manual?" will often get them off your back.**

98. Take yourself seriously, but never take your job seriously.

99. Convey the impression that your company has offices all over the world by printing a lot of gobbledygook on the back of your business card and telling people they're your Eastern European offices.

100. Belabor your points.

101. Your worth as a person is pretty much determined by your job title.

102. Tell your spouse how to manage his or her career.

103. Forget the little people you step on as you claw your way to the top.

104. Scrimp on the little things (letterhead, business cards, marketing brochures). Those savings will really add up.

105. Make your job sound dangerous. Tell people you've been busy putting out fires, dodging bullets, avoiding poison pills, slaying dragons, juggling greasy chainsaws, and drinking molten lava.

106. Heed astrology warnings. If it says to be wary of Capricorns, don't do business with Capricorns that day. Tell them to come back tomorrow.

107. Add little smiley faces to your business letters.

108. **Some good questions to ask during a job interview are:**

- "What is it that you do at this company?"
- "How many months would I have to work here before I had your job?"
- "Does your company have a concealed weapons policy?"
- "Does your health insurance cover pets?"
- "I have a real problem with capitalism. Is that going to be a problem here?"

109. **Start an office crossword puzzle league or an after-work witches' coven.**

110. Keep troublesome employees in line by threatening to make a note in their "permanent record."

111. Formulate an "all-your-eggs-in-one-basket," single-career strategy.

112. Send your boss a ten thousand dollar purchase request for Louis XIV office furnishings. If he calls you on it, say it was a joke. If it goes through by mistake—hey, nice office.

113. Praise in private. Reprimand in public.

114. Buy one share of stock in your company. Whenever the stock goes down, call the CEO and tell him that as a stockholder, he is accountable to you and you are very disappointed in him.

115. Just for laughs, make your boss look bad in front of her boss.

116. **Boss around anyone hired after you, regardless of their position.**

☎

117. **Keep your supervisor off your back with retorts like "I answer to a higher authority" and "You're not the boss of me."**

118. **Don't bother learning the names of people you may never see again. Wait until you've met them five times to be sure it's worth the effort.**

119. Buy high. Sell low.

120. In staff meetings, every couple of minutes say, "I move that we table the discussion and proceed to the next order of business" to demonstrate your command of Robert's Rules of Order.

121. Start a staple recycling program.

122. If the copier jams while you're using it, bolt.

123. **Treat secretaries like dirt. After all, they're only secretaries. What can they do?**

124. **Convince your boss your pay is too low by constantly asking him if you can borrow some money.**

125. **Spell-checking software eats up a lot of valuable hard-disk space. Don't bother with it.**

126. Express all calculations in obscure units of measurement (i.e., instead of "feet per second" use "leagues per blue moon").

☎

127. Rifle through colleagues' in-boxes. You never know what valuable gems they've been sitting on. If you take anything, though, be courteous and leave them a note.

128. If at first you don't succeed, try something easier.

129. **Instead of cash tips, give waiters, barbers, and cab drivers "inside information" on your company's stock and tell them to make their own money.**

130. **Rest on your laurels.**

131. **When you come back from sick leave and your nosy boss asks what you had, tell him: "I was just so sick of seeing your puffy face, monkey-boy."**

132. Pay early. Bill late.

133. In proposals, say you are going to use Nobel prize-winning scientists to do the job. Once you've won the contract, hire a bunch of college interns to do it instead.

134. Great leaders are a dime a dozen. Strive to be a great manager instead.

135. Keep employees in the dark about company financial performance. It's none of their business.

136. Keep your desk messy so you look busy to others.

137. On "National Bring Our Daughters to Work Day" give a talk entitled "Warning to Career Women of Tomorrow: Play by Men's Rules or Else!"

138. **Only return calls to people who leave four or more messages.**

139. **Clean your file cabinets by throwing out every third folder regardless of its contents.**

140. **Fool your boss into thinking you worked late the previous night by leaving notes on her desk with fake times like 11:30 P.M.**

141. Address your memos to "All Those Who Obey My Commands" and see who really listens to you.

142. The day your "new hire probationary period" expires, start goofing off. They can't touch you now.

143. Remember: arrogance and likability go hand in hand.

144. Finish other people's sentences for them.

145. Tell your staff not to think of you as a boss, but as a fellow colleague—a colleague who just happens to be right all the time.

146. When tasked with a particularly difficult job, get yourself off the hook with a simple, "No thanks, Attila. That job is beneath me. Find some other lackey to do your dirty work."

147. Eliminate shoplifting by frisking customers on their way out.

148. Motivate employees by awarding them gold stars on the lunchroom refrigerator for jobs well done.

149. Earn extra money by selling your customer lists to competitors.

150. Skip breakfast. Skip lunch. Grab candy bars from the vending machine for a quick pick-me-up.

151. Don't associate with "cubicle dwellers."

152. Communicate only as a last resort. Instead rely on hunches, impressions, and mental telepathy.

153. Deliver projects late and over budget. They expect it and nobody likes a goody-goody.

154. Every day arrive at work five seconds later and leave five seconds earlier. The daily change will be imperceptible to everyone. Done properly over time, you should be able to avoid work entirely and still collect your pay.

155. Impress your boss with your dedication to work by calling her at home during the night and on weekends to ask job-related questions, like "What account code do I put in box seven of a purchase order for more pens?"

156. If being a hard-ass doesn't get the job done, try being a harder-ass.

157. The longer the memo, the better.

158. Don't neglect the many lucrative business opportunities that may accrue to your company by doing business with organized crime.

159. Swearing at work shows you are tough.

160. Give your next budget presentation using a sock-puppet. Introduce it as "Baxter P. McGruff, the bean-counting billy-goat."

161. **Invoice clients twice for the same work. Every once in a while they'll pay double.**

162. **Don't waste time networking. It's just a bunch of hype.**

163. **If your staff presents you with new ideas, keep 'em in line with, "Hey, if I had wanted creativity, I would have asked my accountant. You're a doer, not a thinker. Get back to work."**

164. **Pirate software.**

165. **There is no sweeter sound that the sound of your own voice talking endlessly at meetings.**

166. **Be cavalier with proprietary information.**

167. **Ignore the career path that attracts you the most. It is a chimera.**

168. Refer to "staff meetings" as "staff infections" and "org charts" as "orgasm charts."

169. Instead of putting Muzak on your phone hold system like everyone else, try something different like rap or heavy metal.

170. You are solely responsible for your successes. Your boss and your staff conspire every morning to produce your failures.

171. At the company Christmas party, go wild. Dance the Macarena with your boss's wife. Chug beers while standing on your head. Everyone expects it.

172. If a colleague touches your arm while making a point, recoil in horror, shout "bad touch," and file a sexual harassment suit.

173. In negotiations, seek win-lose outcomes.

174. **If you're in danger of being fired, scare them into keeping you by making comments about how you're on the verge of going "postal."**

175. **Put all your calls on speakerphone at full blast.**

176. When your boss asks how you like your job, tell him, "It'll pay the bills until I sell my movie deal about a corporate whistleblower who discovers his boss is embezzling money, strangles him, and then runs off with the boss's lusty wife."

177. Make yourself seem computer literate by adding "dot com" to the end of everything you say dot com.

178. Treat those below you on the org chart like depraved, leprous subhumanoids, knowing that they would do the same to you if the roles were reversed.

☎

179. Most letters are too long. Coin your own acronyms like IRTYLDFN for "In response to your letter dated February 9th" and YOWBPBTEONW for "Your order will be processed by the end of next week."

180. Only use the bathroom in that obscure part of the building and be real secretive about it.

181. Don't end business letters with a boring "Sincerely." For variety, try closing with "Whatever," "Yada Yada Yada," or "And So On and So Forth."

182. Tell your boss to suck a breath mint before he talks to you.

183. Remember: authority is only given, never taken.

184. Be indecisive, noncommittal, and vague when giving instructions to subordinates.

185. At 5:00 P.M. shout "Yabba-dabba-doo! It's quittin' time!"

186. **Strong-arm people into giving to the United Way, participating in the company blood drive, and buying candy bars for your kid's soccer team.**

187. **Ask permission before proceeding with anything.**

188. **Let a full coffeepot stand on the burner overnight until the water evaporates. Next morning scrape dried coffee dust into a mug, add hot water, and treat your boss to "espresso."**

189. **The passive voice should be used in business writing.**

190. **Store magnets near your floppy disks. Magnetic media should be kept together.**

191. **Encourage "group-think" to reach consensus.**

192. Drive human resources people batty with job application responses like, "Under no obligation to answer question. Court docket sealed."

193. Turn a cost center into a profit center by replacing your 1-800 number with a 1-900 number.

194. Start a chain letter on the office e-mail system.

195. During explanations of corporate reorganizations, shout "The emperor has no clothes!"

196. Surfing the net on company time is a good way to appear busy.

197. No memo is complete without a bibliography, index, footnotes, and dedication.

198. Post *Dilbert* cartoons on your office door and write on them: "So true! That's how stupid my idiot boss is!"

199. So what if you take the last cup of coffee. They don't pay you those big bucks to fuss around with coffee machines. Let someone else do it.

200. Complain, whine, and moan.

201. Motivate employees by frequently reminding them how dispensable they are. Refer to them as ERHUs, short for Easily Replaceable Humanoid Units.

202. If your job sucks, stay at it until it stops sucking.

203. Compromise your principles if you must; but never, ever change your opinions.

204. If you want to leave work early, microwave popcorn until it catches fire. The rude smell will encourage everyone to bail ASAP.

205. Give subordinates instructions and ask them to repeat them back to you. When they are repeated change them slightly. When they are repeated again, change them again. On the third time, say, "You just don't get it, do you?"

206. **Deadlines are a misnomer. Is anyone really going to die if that report isn't done by a certain date?**

207. **Take credit for other people's ideas.**

208. **Treat summer interns like your own personal serfs. Have them pick up your dry cleaning, fetch lunch, wash your car.**

209. **The most important thing in life is to secure ever-larger offices and desks.**

210. TYPE ENTIRE MEMOS IN ALL CAPS. THE SAME GOES FOR E-MAIL.

211. Send hundred-page faxes.

212. To conquer stage fright when giving a business presentation, imagine your audience buck naked. Tell them you are doing this so they will understand if you get aroused.

213. **Tell your staff that you want to be treated the way "Smithers" treats "Mr. Burns" on *The Simpsons*.**

214. **If someone submits their resignation, try to talk them out of it. Then fire them.**

215. **Play petty office politics.**

216. Leave incriminating unsigned "While You Were Out" slips lying around for rival co-workers: "Eric, your bookie returned your call," "Laura, lab called re: syphilis test," "Todd, Narcotics Anonymous meeting canceled."

217. Sit in the back of the room during meetings. Your napping is less noticeable there.

218. **If you receive a letter of complaint from a customer, write them back a curt note saying you'll do just fine without their business.**

219. **Cultivate a stern look at work.**

220. **Don't waste time checking your computer for viruses. They're just a myth.**

221. A colleague is out for the day. You're rummaging through her desk because you need her folder on the XYZ project. Don't be in such a hurry to find it that you skip browsing through other, more interesting files, such as "Performance Reviews," "Pay Stubs," "Medical Claims," and "Personal."

☎

222. If employees do not perform well, give them a "time out" and make them sit quietly in an empty room until they are ready to work hard.

223. Place best-selling business books in conspicuous places in your office. People will think you've read these dry tomes, but you know better.

224. Leave work one minute after your boss leaves.

225. Believe what you read in the newspapers.

226. Do nothing all day. Then, at 4:59 P.M., dump a big load of work on your secretary.

227. Never overlook the amusement value of the simple act of faxing a photocopy of your buttocks to the branch offices.

228. When flying, always request special meals. Tell the airline you are on a special doctor-ordered "lobster, champagne, and raspberries diet."

229. Don't learn coworkers' names. Acknowledge them in the hall with meaningless jive like "There he is," "Hey, big guy," and "Duuuuude."

230. Skirt the chain of command.

231. If work matters find you asking yourself, "Is it worth going to jail over this?" console yourself with the thought, "At least I face exciting dilemmas."

232. You'll never get what you want. Don't look stupid by asking for it.

233. When people get fired, keep your distance from them. It can be contagious.

234. **Spend your whole life making other people rich.**

235. **Weed out unimportant calls by answering the phone with a suspicious, challenging air to your voice.**

236. **If a colleague asks you to car-pool, laugh at him and say, "Like I don't see enough of you in the office!"**

237. **Be noticed. CC: the company president on all your memos.**

238. **Ignore body language. It's just a bunch of sociological drivel.**

239. **If you don't know what to say in a meeting and are asked your opinion, try saying, "This is all well and good, but have you examined the implications of the information superhighway on this?"**

240. Promise your boss the world. Deliver whatever. He's got a short memory.

241. Carry a big bag of negativity wherever you go.

242. When doing business internationally, avoid conforming to local customs. It's just not the American way.

243. It is more important to talk than to listen.

244. **Insist that everyone always put everything in writing.**

245. **Frame every diploma and certificate you've ever received and hang them prominently in your office.**

246. **Treat independent contractors and outside consultants better than your own employees.**

247. **Form cliques at work and shun outsiders.**

248. Every day when you get to work, get motivated to succeed by asking yourself, "Ohmigod, is this all I've amounted to? Is this really how I am spending my precious life?"

249. Thank-you notes are archaic. Nobody uses them in business anymore.

250. Be a perfectionist in all things, big and small.

251. Leap to conclusions.

252. Start useless corporate initiatives with meaningless names like the "Zero-Defect Total Quality Management and Customer Service Program."

253. Remember: projects always take less time than you think.

254. Always shake hands limply. The person will think you are weak and underestimate you.

255. Report any employee you suspect of violating company policy.

256. When delegating work to others, follow this handy four-step plan:

- **tell them the task**
- **tell them exactly how to do it**
- **spoon-feed them little bits of information**
- **ask them to regurgitate the information back to you**

257. **Give your staff responsibility for outcomes without authority for implementation.**

258. **If someone doesn't appear to be listening, talk louder and louder until they do.**

259. **Pick a slogan to use every day, like, "Let's run that idea up the flagpole and see who salutes" or "Make it happen."**

260. Declare yourself a "free agent" in the next company staff meeting and ask the department heads to bid for you.

261. Flip your tie over your shoulder during a business lunch so you don't spill food on it. Then say, "Look at me. I'm the Red Baron!"

262. Lose sight of the trees while gazing at the forest.

263. Every day ask yourself, "What can my company do for me today?"

264. Make your voice-mail system a voice-*jail* system.

265. Speak decisively if you are sure of yourself. Speak hesitantly if you are unsure of yourself.

266. Question authority. Your boss's, for example.

267. Create momentum for new initiatives by kicking them off with a memorable beginning. For example, to start a drive to eliminate corporate "red tape," hire an actor to play a bureaucrat and have everyone stone him.

268. Handle every piece of paper many times before dealing with it.

269. Since most meetings are a waste of time, don't go. If they really need you, they'll give you a special invitation.

270. At annual bonus time, most people would prefer a handsome honorary plaque instead of vile cash money.

271. Take work home with you. Think about your most difficult work problems during family time. Your subconscious mind will help you solve the problem.

☎

272. Refuse any task that's not in your job description.

273. Innovation is overrated. If it's such a great idea, why hasn't anyone else thought of it before?

274. Talk a big game.

275. Thumb your nose at Murphy's Law.

276. Inform your staff that working overtime every day and on weekends is the only way to get ahead.

277. Scoff at other people's ideas in brainstorming sessions.

278. Schedules are for idiots. In the time you waste making a schedule, you could be well into the project.

279. Brag about your sexual conquests at work.

280. Not finishing your daily "to-do" list is so depressing, so be sure to load it with some easy ones: "get out of bed in morning," "breathe at least twice per minute," "avoid costing company $1 billion in derivative losses," etc.

281. Cook the books.

282. People like to be noticed. Comment on their funny accents, receding hairlines, tight skirts, and other distinguishing characteristics.

283. Believe your own press releases.

284. Greet everyone getting on the company elevator with a warm handshake and wish them a pleasant ride.

285. After salary and bonus reviews, ask others how they did.

286. Cop an "us vs. them" attitude.

287. If you run out of stuff to do, ask your boss if your work hours can be reduced to accommodate your less than full workload.

288. Work hard, not smart.

289. Times Roman be damned! Do your memos in FONTS that reflect your INDIVIDUALITY.

290. Save every single piece of paper you get. You never know what might be important later.

291. If an interviewer asks you "What is your biggest weakness," say "What is this? A freakin' inquisition? I'm outta here. I don't have to answer questions like that." Somebody's got to draw the line with these guys.

☎

292. Cultivate a "me boss, you slave" work environment.

293. Think of your family primarily as a career asset.

294. Liven things up at the next boring meeting by staring glassy-eyed at the person next to you and shouting in a demonic voice, "I must find a more suitable host body!"

295. Hog both armrests on airplanes.

296. Remember: the company is lucky to have you. There's a helluva lot of jobs out there.

297. Say "I'm sorry" a lot.

298. **Handy rule for giving presentations:**

- **tell 'em what you're going to tell 'em**
- **tell 'em what you're *not* going to tell 'em**
- **tell 'em what you think they want to hear**

299. **It's better to produce a high volume of low-quality work than a low volume of high-quality work.**

300. During job interviews, ask about perks like orthodontic coverage, sabbaticals, tuition reimbursement, stock options, maternity leave, workout facilities, day care, mental health benefits, Christmas bonuses, and carpal-tunnel-syndrome disability pay. Boast that you plan to avail yourself of all the "goodies" they have to offer.

301. If you fail at one thing, ask yourself what makes you think you'll succeed at the next thing.

302. When giving a business presentation, rattle off your pitch with a determined air. But as soon as they start asking you questions, panic and become disoriented.

☎

303. If a colleague is frustrated, cheer him up by telling him that in thirty years or less he'll probably be dead and whatever is bugging him won't matter anymore.

304. Talk to people at work like you would talk to a very small child.

305. Snoop around the accounting offices after hours. They often leave out sensitive salary information that could come in handy.

306. Always have a back-up plan. For example, if your project fails, your back-up plan can be: "I'll be fired, lose my home and my family, live in a refrigerator box under the bridge, and curse the day I was born."

307. When you're under stress, take a deep breath, count to ten . . . then panic.

308. Speak off the cuff with the media.

309. When you leave a job, go out with a bang. Burn your bridges and tell them what you really think of them.

310. Hoard information.

311. When working on a special corporate "team," propose that the first order of business be the design of a team logo and composition of a team "victory song."

312. Play fast and loose with your time-sheet hours.

☎

313. Business plans are for wimps.

314. Replace your boss's erasable white board markers with permanent Magic Markers.

315. Before starting a home-based business it is wise to spend several years researching zoning laws, local tax and license requirements, municipal regulations, and home-based business restrictions.

316. Smiling while talking on the phone makes you sound like a bozo. Frown instead.

317. Win sympathy in job interviews by discussing your personal and financial problems.

318. Talk about sensitive business matters in the restroom without checking to see who is in the other stalls.

319. The world owes you.

320. When someone enters your office, glance up furtively and shuffle papers around as if you're hiding something.

321. Spread rumors about imaginary impending layoffs.

322. **Propose that the "Corporate Mission Statement" be rewritten to say, "This company exists for the sole purpose of maximizing the happiness and financial well-being of [*insert your name here*]."**

323. **People skills are a crock.**

324. **Rough rule of thumb for presentations: thirty minutes per chart.**

325. Use excess verbiage to disguise your inaction: "I am presently in the option-formulation stage of my problem resolution mode."

326. Speed through the company parking lot.

327. Change your company's name periodically.

328. When talking to a client who rambles a lot, say, "Well, enough about your needs. Let me tell you what we offer."

329. **Never admit you are wrong.**

330. **Whoever has time to make nasty little signs for the company lunchroom saying "Your mother doesn't work here" has a lot of spare time on her hands. Let her clean up your mess.**

331. **Don't waste time "marketing" when you could be working on your "marketing plan."**

332. Adopt the habits of highly slothful people.

☎

333. Charge people a nickel for printing costs when you give them your business card.

334. Practice the KISS philosophy: *Keep Intimidating Stupid Subordinates.*

335. Call a meeting for no reason. When people show up, say you were "lonely and bored and didn't want to work and just wanted to talk to a bunch of people about a bunch of stuff."

336. Once you get a job, celebrate by burning your résumé. Won't be needing that sucker anymore.

337. Judge people at work not by their accomplishments, but by their knowledge of sports.

338. Post parodies of corporate memos on your door.

339. When someone speaks to you, don't let the sound of their voice disturb your thinking about what you are going to say as soon as they shut up.

340. Criticize rather than empathize.

341. Take the first job that comes along.

342. When your boss is giving you instructions, tell him to go away, put it in writing, then hand it to you. When he returns, be hard to find.

☎

343. Making it known that you are looking for a new job is a good way to pressure them into treating you better.

344. Punctuality, schmunctuality.

345. When exchanging phone messages with someone, tell them something hilarious and original, like, "Hey, we're playing phone tag!"

346. Instead of simply managing chaos, create it.

347. Repeating the same work over and over again is the key to job security.

348. Hard disks are easily damaged by saving documents too frequently. It is best to wait until the document is finished before saving.

349. Begin every letter with the universal, all-purpose beginning, "Per your request, please find enclosed the following letter from me to you concerning the topic of . . ."

350. Contribute to "shrinkage."

351. Expect your organization to repay your love and loyalty.

352. Cushion the blow of firing somebody by prefacing your remarks with, "Jim, regrettably, circumstances beyond my control have forced me to sign your death warrant."

353. Be afraid to ask "dumb" questions.

354. Do pleasant tasks first. Leave the unpleasant ones for later. Who knows? They might go away.

355. Inflate your salary history.

356. Ask interviewees if they would take a bullet for the president of the company.

357. Leave the quaint notion of "business ethics" to the ivory-tower types.

358. Resent the success and good fortune of others. It should be yours.

359. Prices are only negotiable if they say they're negotiable.

360. Think of employees as "units of production."

361. The best way to find a job is through the classified ads.

362. Show up at your company's Toastmasters meeting with a loaf of bread and a stick of butter and act really confused.

363. Learn the difference between being assertive and being aggressive. Then be aggressive.

364. **Give your file folders descriptive names like "Boring Thing for Marty," "Budget Lies," "Tom's Nasty Project," or "Schedule Crap."**

365. **Write stupid little books on company time.**

EPILOGUE

If you have a ridiculous maxim or observation about the business world, don't send it to Scott Adams. E-mail it to me: stevealtes@aol.com.

ABOUT THE AUTHOR

It didn't take a rocket scientist to write this book. No, wait. Actually, it did. Steve Altes, 34, has three degrees in aerospace engineering from the Massachusetts Institute of Technology. His eclectic career path has involved stints as a professional scuba diver, congressional staffer, model, aide to the President of the United States, management consultant, rocket scientist, stand-in for Brad Pitt, and trainer at the FBI Academy.

He is a corecipient of the 1991 National Medal of Technology (the nation's highest award for engineering achievement) and the Smithsonian's National Air and Space Museum Trophy. Steve's first book, *The Aerospace Plane: Technological Feasibility and Policy Implications* (MIT, 1986), was a real snorefest.